A POC...

STATIONS
OF THE
CROSS

According to the method of St. Alphonsus Liguori

KEVIN AND MARY O'NEILL
BUILDING BLOCKS OF FAITH SERIES

SOPHIA INSTITUTE PRESS

Manchester, New Hampshire

Sophia Institute Press

Box 5284, Manchester, NH 03108

1-800-888-9344

www.SophiaInstitute.com

Sophia Institute Press® is a registered trademark of Sophia Institute.

print ISBN: 978-1-64413-880-9

ebook ISBN: 978-1-64413-881-6

Library of Congress Control Number: 2022948452

THE STATIONS OF THE CROSS

According to the Method of St. Alphonsus Liguori

"Let each one, kneeling before the high altar, make an Act of Contrition, and form the intention of gaining the indulgences connected to this devotion, whether for himself or for the souls in Purgatory."

Act of Contrition

O my God, I am heartily sorry for having offended You, and I detest all my sins because I dread the loss of Heaven and the pains of hell, but most of all because they have offended You, my God, who art all good and deserving of all my love. I firmly resolve, with the help of Your grace, to confess my sins, to do penance, and to amend my life. Amen.

Preparatory Prayer

My Lord Jesus Christ, You have made this journey to die for me with love unutterable, and I have so many times unworthily abandoned You; but now I love You with my whole heart, and because I love You, I repent sincerely for ever having offended You. Pardon me, my God, and permit me to accompany You on this journey. You goest to die for love of me; I wish also, my beloved Redeemer, to die for love of You. My Jesus, I will live and die always united to You.

INSTRUCTIONS

At each station:

1. The leader (or priest) announces the station.

2. The leader says: "We adore You, O Christ, and we praise You."

3. The people respond: "Because by Your holy Cross, You have redeemed the world."

4. The leader leads the reflection.

5. The people read the response.

6. They pray together: one Our Father, one Hail Mary, and one Glory Be prayer.

7. The leader and the people finish each station with: "Jesus, for You I live, Jesus, for You I die, Jesus, I am Yours in life and in death. Amen."

Leader: We adore You, O Christ, and we praise You.

People: Because by Your holy Cross, You have redeemed the world.

Leader: Consider how Jesus, after having been scourged and crowned with thorns, was unjustly condemned by Pilate to die on the Cross.

People: My adorable Jesus, it was not Pilate, no, it was my sins that condemned You to die. I beseech You, by the merits of this sorrowful journey, to assist my soul in its journey towards eternity. I love You, my beloved Jesus; I love You more than myself; I repent with my whole heart of having offended You. Never permit me to separate myself from You again. Grant that I may love You always; and then do with me what You will.

All: Our Father, Hail Mary, Glory Be

All: Jesus, for You I live, Jesus, for You I die, Jesus, I am Yours in life and in death. Amen.

Leader: We adore You, O Christ, and we praise You.

People: Because by Your holy Cross, You have redeemed the world.

Leader: Consider how Jesus, in making this journey with the Cross on His shoulders thought of us, and for us offered to His Father the death that He was about to undergo.

People: My most beloved Jesus, I embrace all the tribulations You have destined for me until death. I beseech You, by the merits of the pain You suffered in carrying Your Cross, to give me the necessary help to carry mine with perfect patience, and resignation. I love You, Jesus my love; I repent of having offended You. Never permit me to separate myself from You again. Grant that I may love You always; and then do with me what You will.

All: Our Father, Hail Mary, Glory Be

All: Jesus, for You I live, Jesus, for You I die, Jesus, I am Yours in life and in death. Amen.

Leader: We adore You, O Christ, and we praise You.

People: Because by Your holy Cross, You have redeemed the world.

Leader: Consider this first fall of Jesus under His Cross. His flesh was torn by the scourges, His head crowned with thorns, and He had lost a great quantity of blood. He was so weakened that he could scarcely walk, and yet He had to carry this great load upon His shoulders. The soldiers struck Him rudely, and thus He fell several times in His journey.

People: My beloved Jesus, it is not the weight of the Cross, but of my sins, which have made You suffer so much pain. Ah, by the merits of this first fall, deliver me from the misfortune of falling into mortal sin. I love You, O my Jesus, with my whole heart; I repent of having offended You. Never permit me to separate myself from You again. Grant that I may love You always; and then do with me what You will.

All: Our Father, Hail Mary, Glory Be

All: Jesus, for You I live, Jesus, for You I die, Jesus, I am Yours in life and in death. Amen.

Leader: We adore You, O Christ, and we praise You.

People: Because by Your holy Cross, You have redeemed the world.

Leader: Consider the meeting of the Son and the Mother, which took place on this journey. Jesus and Mary looked at each other, and their looks became as so many arrows to wound those hearts which loved each other so tenderly.

People: My most loving Jesus, by the sorrow You experienced in this meeting, grant me the grace of a truly devoted love for Your most holy Mother. And You, my Queen, who was overwhelmed with sorrow, obtain for me by Your intercession a continual and tender remembrance of the Passion of Your Son. I love You, Jesus my love; I repent of ever having offended You. Never permit me to offend You again. Grant that I may love You always; and then do with me what You will.

All: Our Father, Hail Mary, Glory Be

All: Jesus, for You I live, Jesus, for You I die, Jesus, I am Yours in life and in death. Amen.

Leader: We adore You, O Christ, and we praise You.

People: Because by Your holy Cross, You have redeemed the world.

Leader: Consider how the Jews, seeing that at each step Jesus from weakness was on the point of expiring, and fearing that He would die on the way, when they wished Him to die the ignominious death of the Cross, constrained Simon the Cyrenian to carry the Cross behind our Lord.

People: My most sweet Jesus, I will not refuse the cross, as the Cyrenian did; I accept it; I embrace it. I accept in particular the death You have destined for me; with all the pains that may accompany it; I unite it to Your death, I offer it to You. You have died for love of me; I will die for love of You, and to please You. Help me by Your grace. I love You, Jesus my love; I repent of having offended You. Never permit me to offend You again. Grant that I may love You always; and then do with me what You will.

All: Our Father, Hail Mary, Glory Be

All: Jesus, for You I live, Jesus, for You I die, Jesus, I am Yours in life and in death. Amen.

Leader: We adore You, O Christ, and we praise You.

People: Because by Your holy Cross, You have redeemed the world.

Leader: Consider how the holy woman named Veronica, seeing Jesus so afflicted, and His face bathed in sweat and blood, presented Him with a towel, with which He wiped His adorable face, leaving on it the impression of His holy countenance.

People: My most beloved Jesus, Your face was beautiful before, but in this journey it has lost all its beauty, and wounds and blood have disfigured it. Alas, my soul also was once beautiful, when it received Your grace in Baptism; but I have disfigured it since by my sins; You alone, my Redeemer, canst restore it to its former beauty. Do this by Your Passion, O Jesus. I repent of having offended You. Never permit me to offend You again. Grant that I may love You always; and then do with me what You will.

All: Our Father, Hail Mary, Glory Be

All: Jesus, for You I live, Jesus, for You I die, Jesus, I am Yours in life and in death. Amen.

Leader: We adore You, O Christ, and we praise You.

People: Because by Your holy Cross, You have redeemed the world.

Leader: Consider the second fall of Jesus under the Cross — a fall which renews the pain of all the wounds of the head and members of our afflicted Lord.

People: My most gentle Jesus, how many times You have pardoned me, and how many times have I fallen again, and begun again to offend You! Oh, by the merits of this new fall, give me the necessary help to persevere in Your grace until death. Grant that in all temptations which assail me I may always commend myself to You. I love You, Jesus my love; I repent of having offended You. Never permit me to offend You again. Grant that I may love You always; and then do with me what You will.

All: Our Father, Hail Mary, Glory Be

All: Jesus, for You I live, Jesus, for You I die, Jesus, I am Yours in life and in death. Amen.

Leader: We adore You, O Christ, and we praise You.

People: Because by Your holy Cross, You have redeemed the world.

Leader: Consider how those women wept with compassion at seeing Jesus in such a pitiable state, streaming with blood, as He walked along. But Jesus said to them: "Weep not for Me, but for your children."

People: My Jesus, laden with sorrows, I weep for the offenses I have committed against You, because of the pains they have deserved, and still more because of the displeasure they have caused You, who have loved me so much. It is Your love, more than the fear of hell, which causes me to weep for my sins. My Jesus, I love You more than myself; I repent of having offended You. Never permit me to offend You again. Grant that I may love You always; and then do with me what You will.

All: Our Father, Hail Mary, Glory Be

All: Jesus, for You I live, Jesus, for You I die, Jesus, I am Yours in life and in death. Amen.

Leader: We adore You, O Christ, and we praise You.

People: Because by Your holy Cross, You have redeemed the world.

Leader: Consider the third fall of Jesus Christ. His weakness was extreme, and the cruelty of His executioners was excessive, who tried to hasten His steps when He had scarcely strength to move.

People: Ah, my outraged Jesus, by the merits of the weakness You suffered in going to Calvary, give me strength sufficient to conquer all human respect, and all my wicked passions, which have led me to despise Your friendship. I love You, Jesus my love, with my whole heart; I repent of having offended You. Never permit me to offend You again. Grant that I may love You always; and then do with me what You will.

All: Our Father, Hail Mary, Glory Be

All: Jesus, for You I live, Jesus, for You I die, Jesus, I am Yours in life and in death. Amen.

Leader: We adore You, O Christ, and we praise You.

People: Because by Your holy Cross, You have redeemed the world.

Leader: Consider the violence with which the executioners stripped Jesus. His inner garments adhered to His torn flesh, and they dragged them off so roughly that the skin came with them. Compassionate your Savior thus cruelly treated, and say to Him:

People: My innocent Jesus, by the merits of the torment You have felt, help me to strip myself of all affection to things of earth, in order that I may place all my love in You, who art so worthy of my love. I love You, O Jesus, with my whole heart; I repent of having offended You. Never permit me to offend You again. Grant that I may love You always; and then do with me what You will.

All: Our Father, Hail Mary, Glory Be

All: Jesus, for You I live, Jesus, for You I die, Jesus, I am Yours in life and in death. Amen.

Leader: We adore You, O Christ, and we praise You.

People: Because by Your holy Cross, You have redeemed the world.

Leader: Consider how Jesus, after being thrown on the Cross extended His hands, and offered to His Eternal Father the sacrifice of His life for our salvation. These barbarians fastened Him with nails, and then, raising the Cross, allowed Him to die with anguish on this infamous gibbet.

People: My Jesus! loaded with contempt, nail my heart to Your feet, that it may ever remain there, to love You, and never quit You again. I love You more than myself; I repent of having offended You. Never permit me to offend You again. Grant that I may love You always; and then do with me what You will.

All: Our Father, Hail Mary, Glory Be

All: Jesus, for You I live, Jesus, for You I die, Jesus, I am Yours in life and in death. Amen.

Leader: We adore You, O Christ, and we praise You.

People: Because by Your holy Cross, You have redeemed the world.

Leader: Consider how Jesus, after three hours' agony on the Cross, consumed at length with anguish, abandons Himself to the weight of His body, bows His head, and dies. (Pause one moment.)

People: O my dying Jesus, I kiss devoutly the Cross on which You died for love of me. I have merited by my sins to die a miserable death; but Your death is my hope. Ah, by the merits of Your death, give me grace to die, embracing Your feet, and burning with love for You. I yield my soul into Your hands. I love You with my whole heart; I repent of ever having offended You. Never permit me to offend You again. Grant that I may love You always; and then do with me what You will.

All: Our Father, Hail Mary, Glory Be

All: Jesus, for You I live, Jesus, for You I die, Jesus, I am Yours in life and in death. Amen.

Leader: We adore You, O Christ, and we praise You.

People: Because by Your holy Cross, You have redeemed the world.

Leader: Consider how, after the death of our Lord, two of His disciples, Joseph and Nicodemus, took Him down from the Cross, and placed Him in the arms of His afflicted Mother, who received Him with unutterable tenderness, and pressed Him to her bosom.

People: O Mother of sorrow, for the love of this Son, accept me for Your servant, and pray to Him for me. And You, my Redeemer, since You have died for me, permit me to love You; for I wish but You, and nothing more. I love You, my Jesus, and I repent of ever having offended You. Never permit me to offend You again. Grant that I may love You always; and then do with me what You will.

All: Our Father, Hail Mary, Glory Be

All: Jesus, for You I live, Jesus, for You I die, Jesus, I am Yours in life and in death. Amen.

Leader: We adore You, O Christ, and we praise You.

People: Because by Your holy Cross, You have redeemed the world.

Leader: Consider how the disciples carried the body of Jesus to bury it, accompanied by His holy Mother, who arranged it in the sepulcher with her own hands. They then closed the tomb, and all withdrew.

People: Oh, my buried Jesus, I kiss the stone that encloses You. But You rose again the third day. I beseech You, by Your Resurrection, make me rise glorious with You at the last day, to be always united with You in heaven, to praise You and love You forever. I love You, and I repent of ever having offended You. Never permit me to offend You again. Grant that I may love You always; and then do with me what You will.

All: Our Father, Hail Mary, Glory Be

All: Jesus, for You I live, Jesus, for You I die, Jesus, I am Yours in life and in death. Amen.

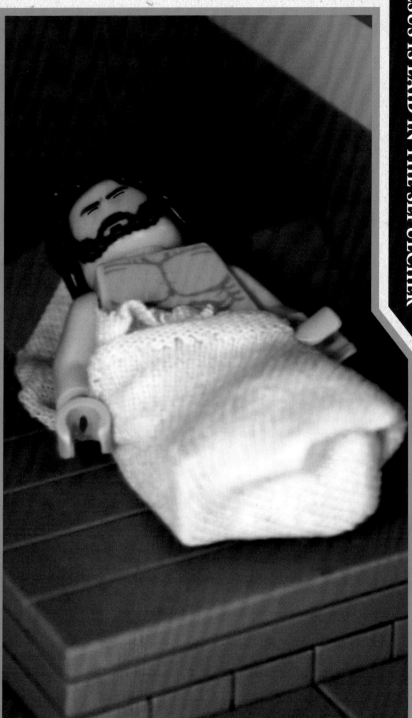

CLOSING PRAYERS

Leader: For the intentions of the Holy Father:

All:

Our Father who art in Heaven, hallowed be Thy Name; Thy Kingdom come; Thy will be done on earth as it is in Heaven. Give us this day our daily bread, and forgive us our trespasses, as we forgive those who trespass against us, and lead us not into temptation, but deliver us from evil. Amen.

Hail Mary, full of grace, the Lord is with thee. Blessed art thou amongst women, and blessed is the fruit of thy womb, Jesus. Holy Mary, Mother of God, pray for us sinners, now and at the hour of our death. Amen.

Glory be to the Father, and to the Son, and to the Holy Spirit, as it was in the beginning, is now, and ever shall be, world without end. Amen.

EXPLORE THE ENTIRE

BUILDING BLOCKS OF FAITH SERIES

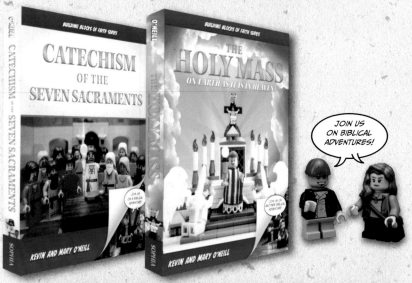

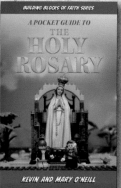

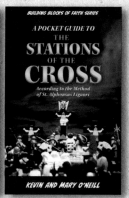

The **Building Blocks of Faith** series works to create and share solidly orthodox materials to help families build their own domestic churches, and, in turn, to build and strengthen the Body of Christ. Our books use typology to explain the foundations of the Faith. We illustrate our graphic novels by building, designing, and photographing intricate sets — built with your child's favorite building-block toys! We strive to spread the Gospel, help the Faith come alive, create disciples, and promote the call to evangelization, as we do our part to build God's Kingdom.

www.sophiainstitute.com/BuildingBlocks